HAL•LEONARD

GUITAR PLAY•ALONG

Christmas carols

VOL. 62

Tracking, mixing, and mastering by Jake Johnson
All guitars by Doug Boduch
French Horn by Mike Szczys
Bass by Tom McGirr
Keyboards by Warren Wiegratz
Drums by Scott Schroedl

ISBN 1-4234-1394-6

Visit Hal Leonard Online at www.halleonard.com

HAL•LEONARD®
CORPORATION
7777 W. BLUEMOUND RD. P.O. BOX 13819
MILWAUKEE, WISCONSIN 53213

CONTENTS

God Rest Ye Merry, Gentlemen

19th Century English Carol

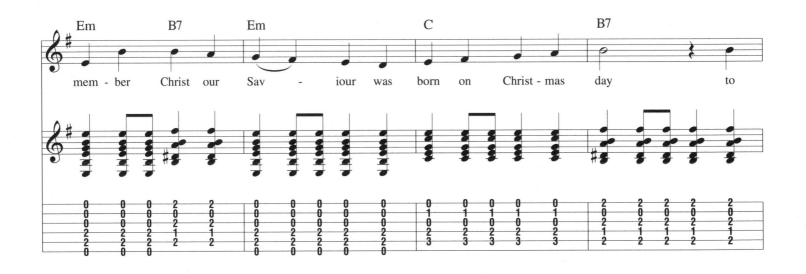

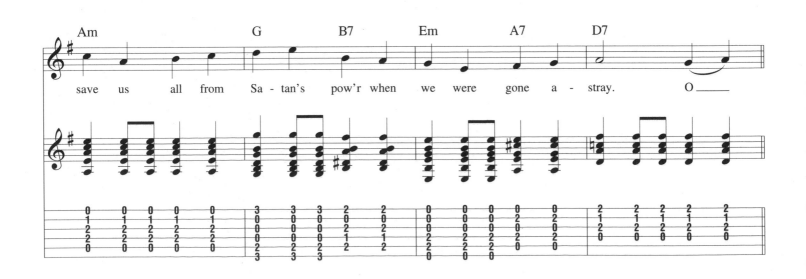

Chorus

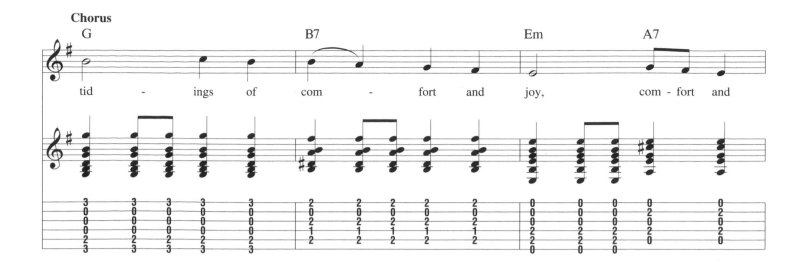

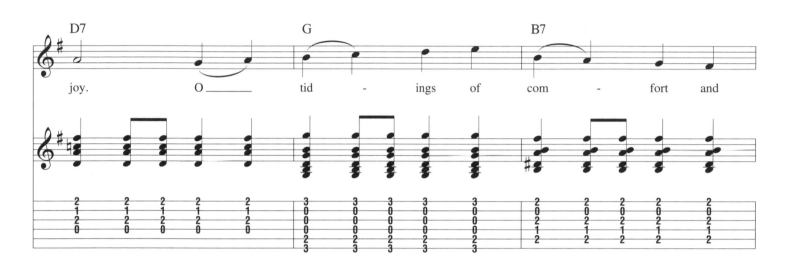

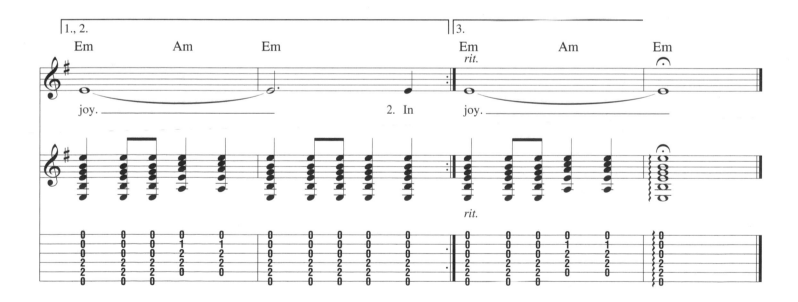

Additional Lyrics

2. In Bethlehem, in Jewry,
   This blessed babe was born,
   And laid within a manger
   Upon this blessed morn
   That which His mother Mary
   Did nothing take in scorn.

3. From God, our Heav'nly Father,
   A blessed angel came,
   And unto certain shepherds
   Brought tidings of the same.
   How that in Bethlehem was born
   The Son of God by name.

Hark! The Herald Angels Sing

Words by Charles Wesley
Altered by George Whitefield
Music by Felix Mendelssohn-Bartholdy

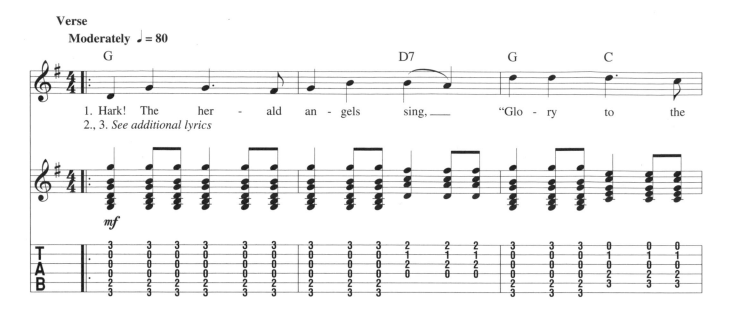

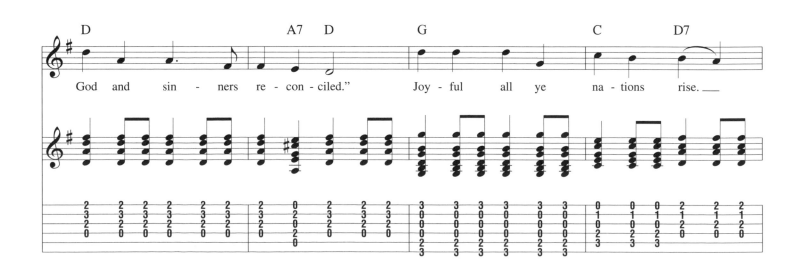

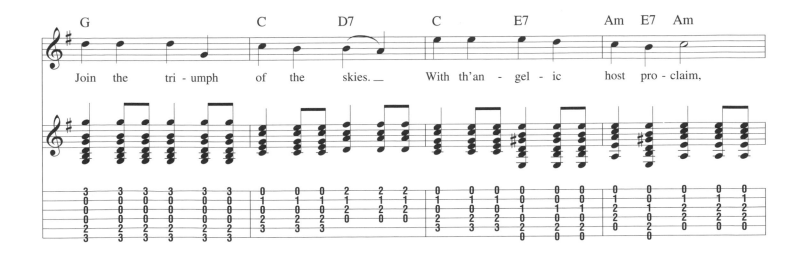

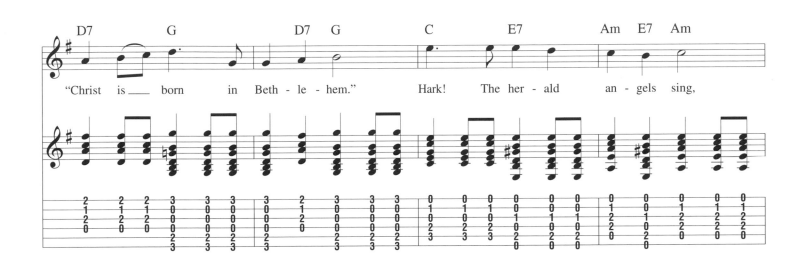

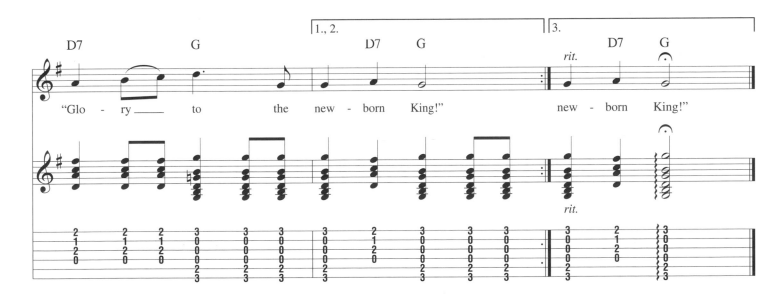

Additional Lyrics

2. Christ, by highest heav'n adored, Christ, the everlasting Lord;
   Late in time behold Him come, offspring of the virgin's womb.
   Veil'd in flesh the Godhead see. Hail th'Incarnate Deity.
   Pleased as man with man to dwell, Jesus our Emmanuel!
   Hark! The herald angels sing, "Glory to the newborn King!"

3. Hail, the heav'n born Prince of Peace! Hail, the Son of Righteousness!
   Light and life to all He brings, ris'n with healing in His wings.
   Mild He lays His glory by. Born that man no more may die.
   Born to raise the sons of earth, born to give them second birth.
   Hark! The herald angels sing, "Glory to the newborn King!"

It Came Upon the Midnight Clear

Words by Edmund H. Sears
Traditional English Melody
Adapted by Arthur Sullivan

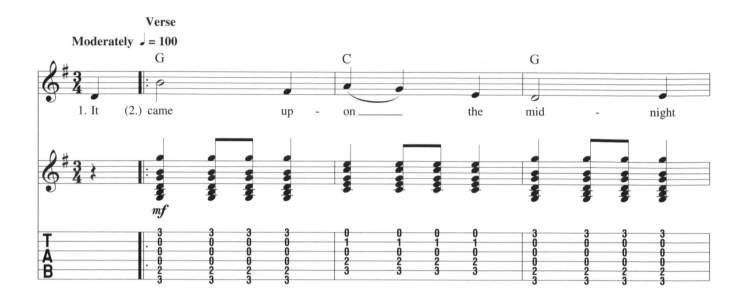

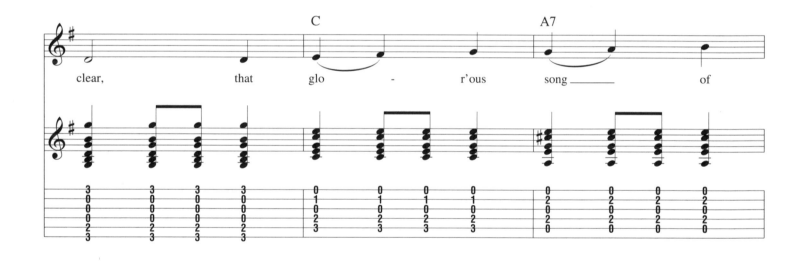

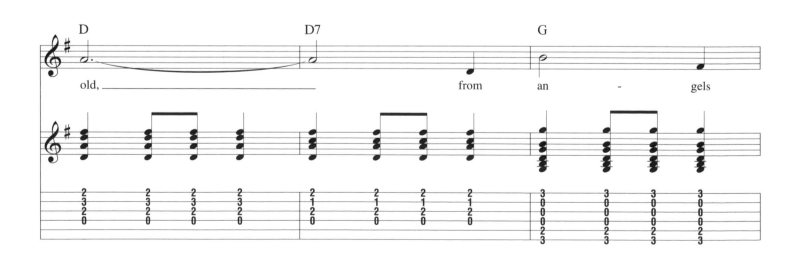

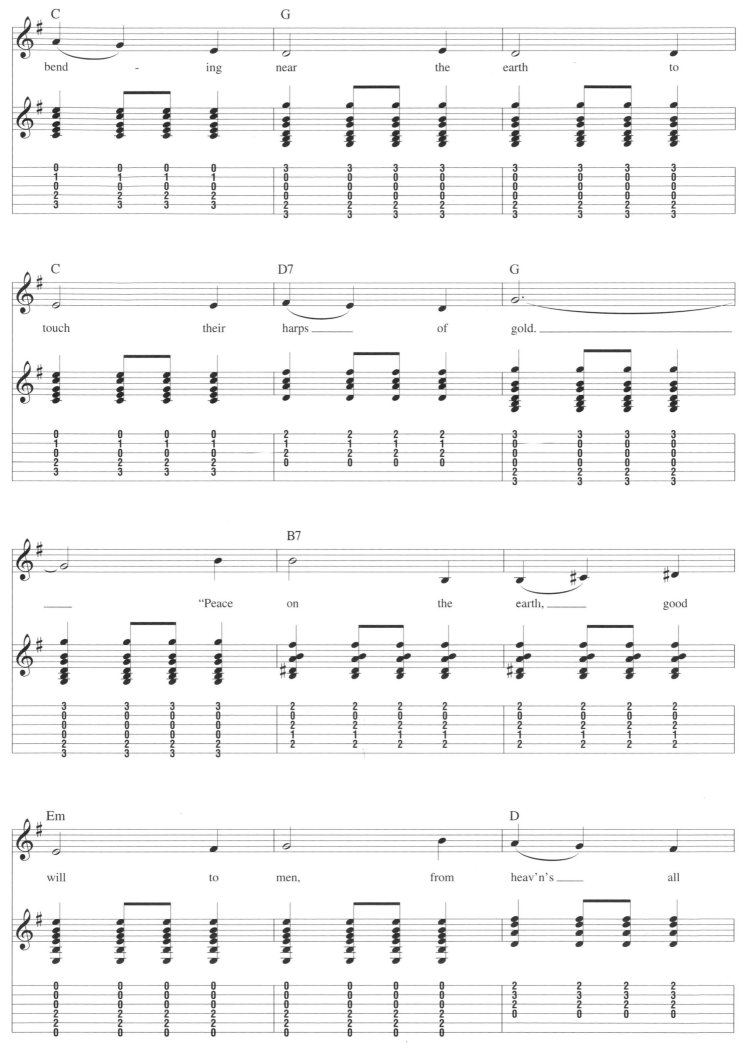

O Holy Night

French Words by Placide Cappeau
English Words by John S. Dwight
Music by Adolphe Adam

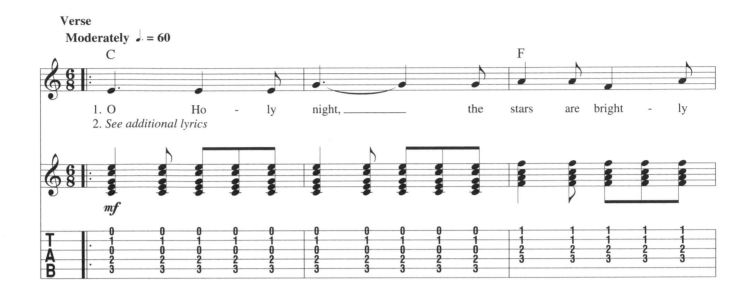

1. O Ho - ly night, _____ the stars are bright - ly
2. *See additional lyrics*

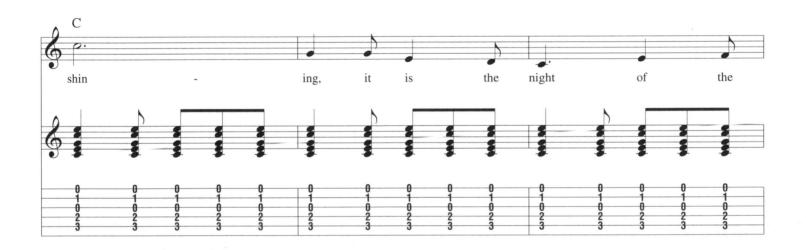

shin - ing, it is the night of the

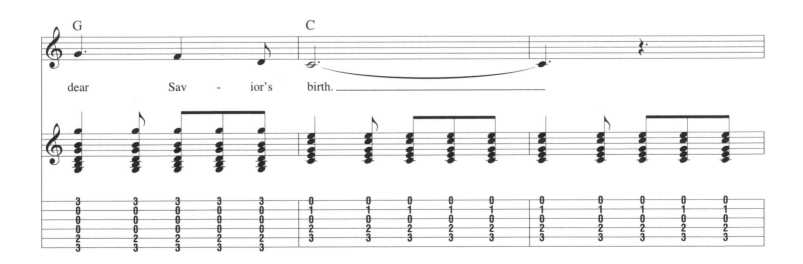

dear Sav - ior's birth. _____

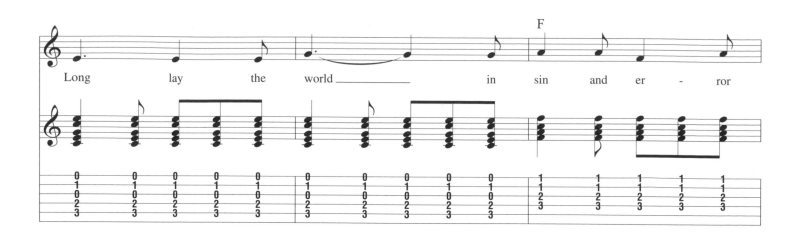

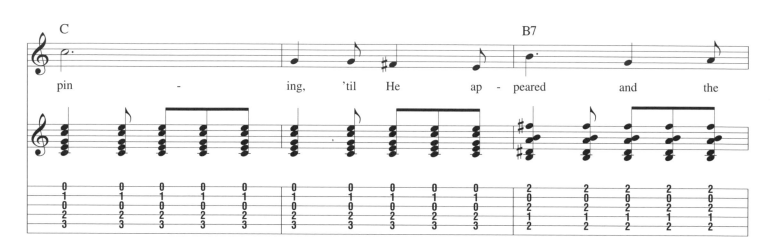

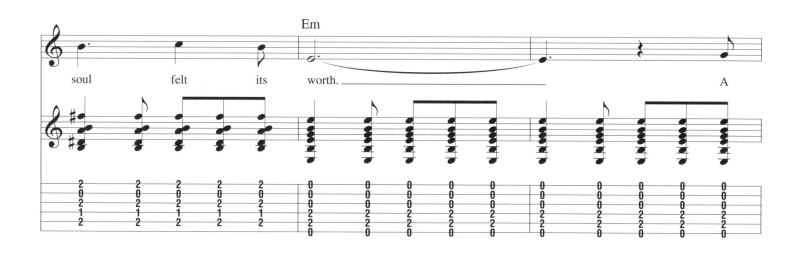

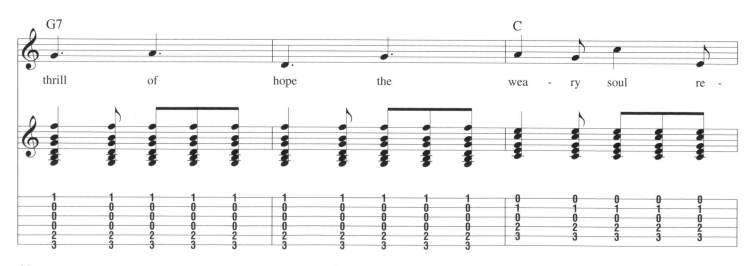

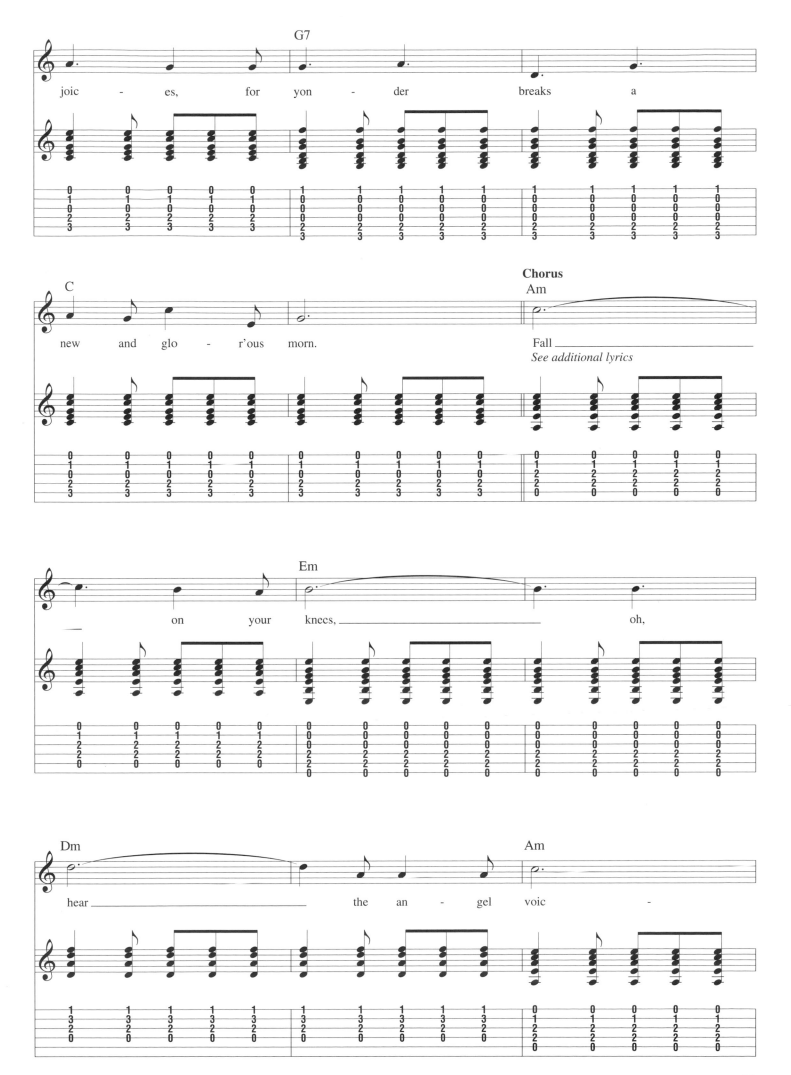

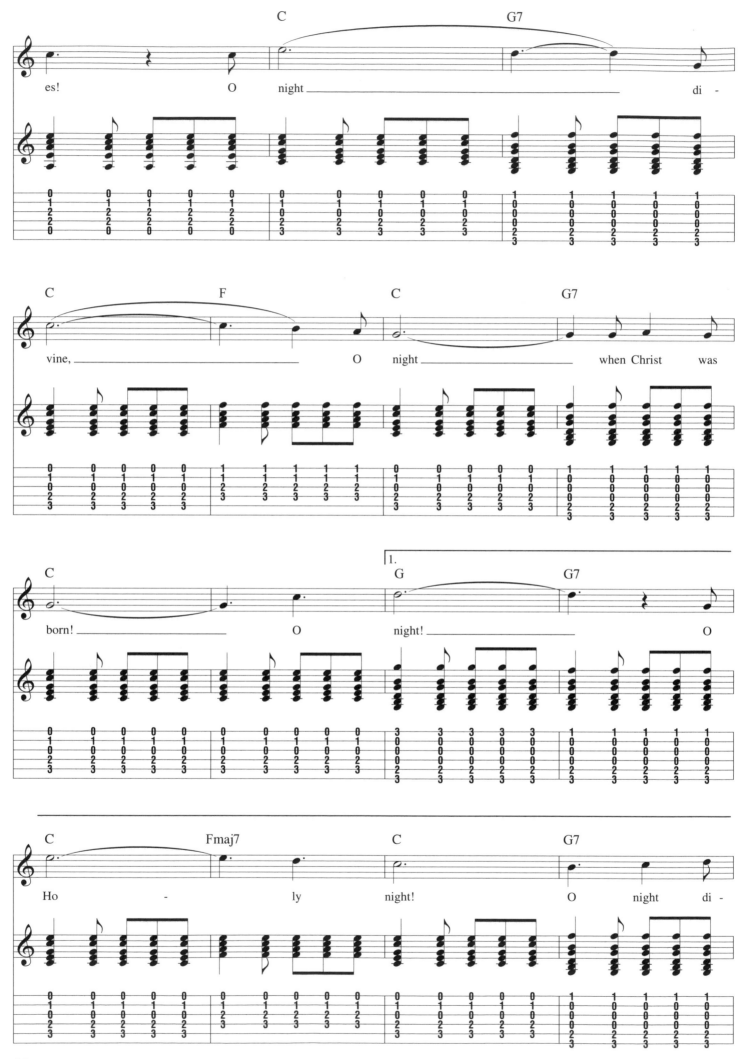

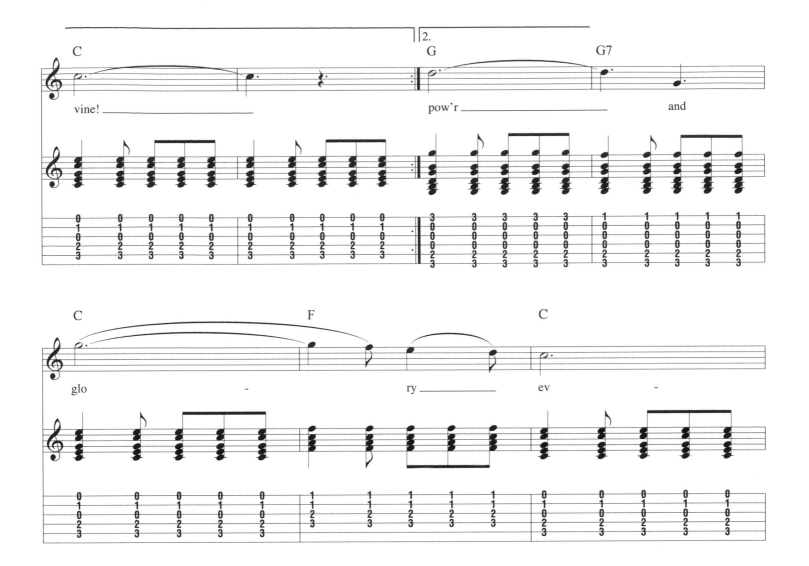

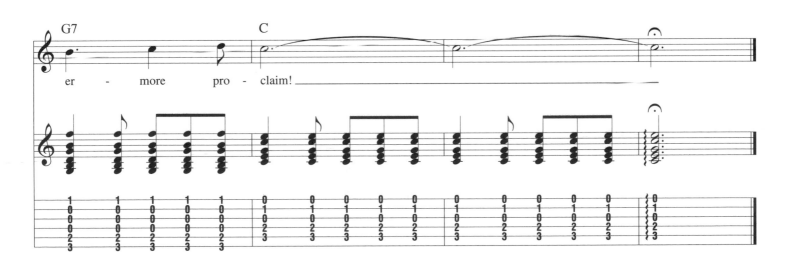

Additional Lyrics

2. Truly He taught us to love one another.
His law is love, and His gospel is peace.
Chains shall He break, for the slave is our brother,
And in His name all oppression shall cease.
Sweet hymns of joy in grateful chorus raise we.
Let all within us praise His holy name.

Chorus Christ is the Lord, oh, praise His name forever!
His pow'r and glory evermore proclaim!
His pow'r and glory evermore proclaim!

O Come, All Ye Faithful
(Adeste Fideles)

Words and Music by John Francis Wade
Latin Words translated by Frederick Oakeley

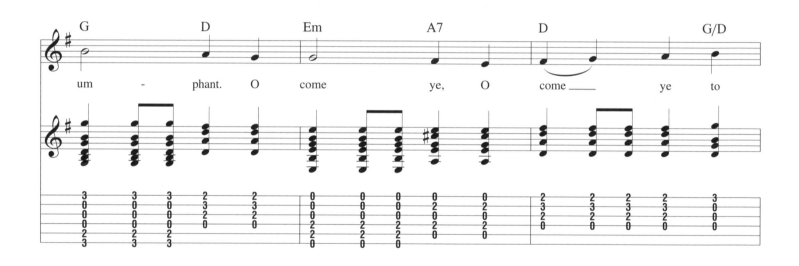

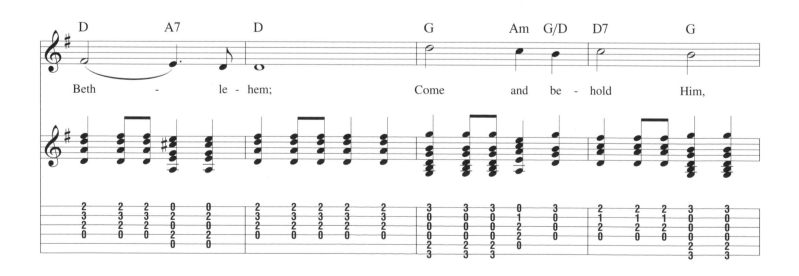

Chorus

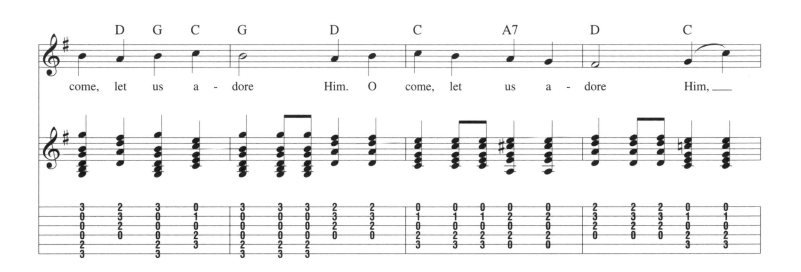

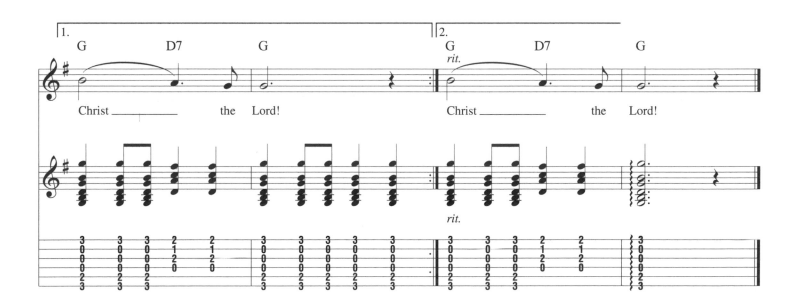

Additional Lyrics

2. Sing choirs of angels, sing in exultation.
O sing all ye citizens of heaven above.
Glory to God in the highest.

Silent Night

Words by Joseph Mohr
Translated by John F. Young
Music by Franz X. Gruber

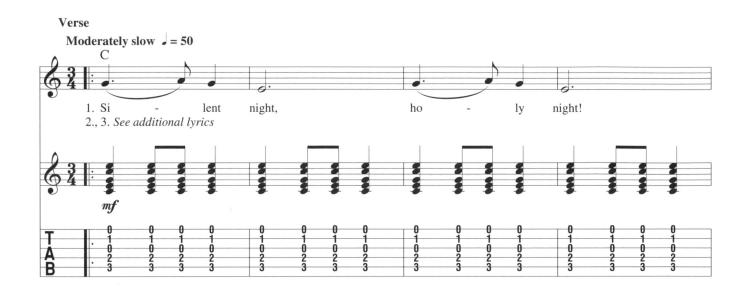

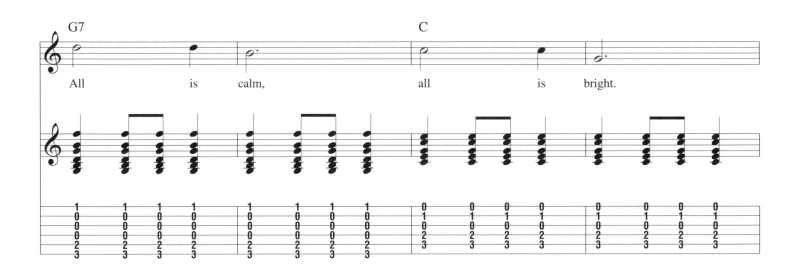

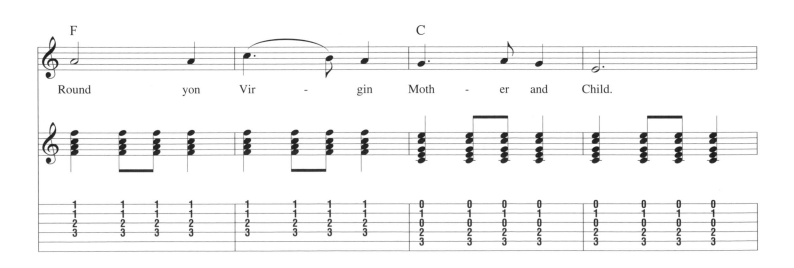

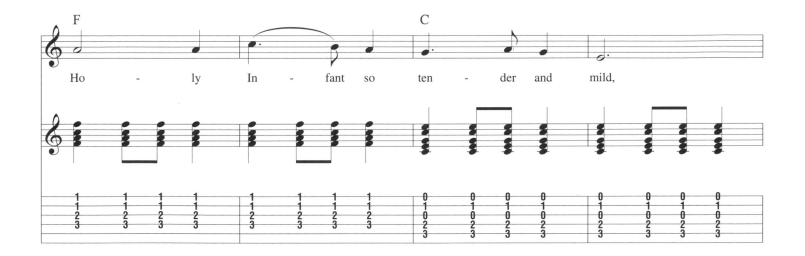

Ho - ly In - fant so ten - der and mild,

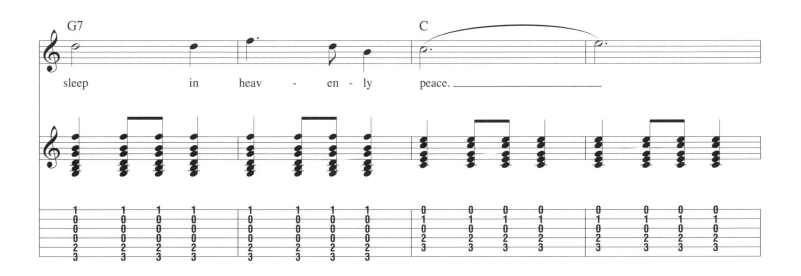

sleep in heav - en - ly peace. _____

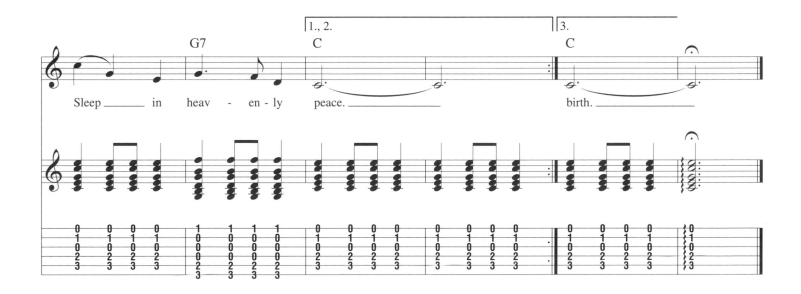

Sleep ____ in heav - en - ly peace. _____ birth. ____

Additional Lyrics

2. Silent night, holy night!
   Shepherds quake at the sight.
   Glories stream from heaven afar.
   Heavenly hosts sing Alleluia.
   Christ the Savior is born!
   Christ the Savior is born!

3. Silent night, holy night!
   Son of God, love's pure light.
   Radiant beams from Thy holy face
   With the dawn of redeeming grace,
   Jesus Lord at Thy birth.
   Jesus Lord at Thy birth.

We Three Kings of Orient Are

Words and Music by John H. Hopkins, Jr.

What Child Is This?

Words by William C. Dix
16th Century English Melody

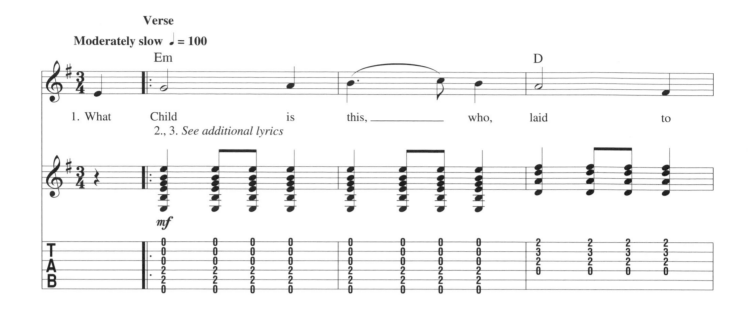

1. What Child is this, who, laid to
2., 3. *See additional lyrics*

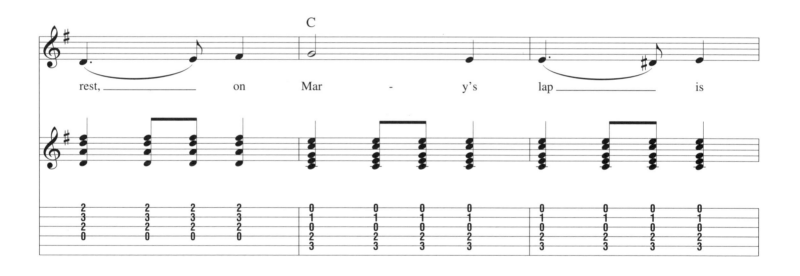

rest, on Mar - y's lap is

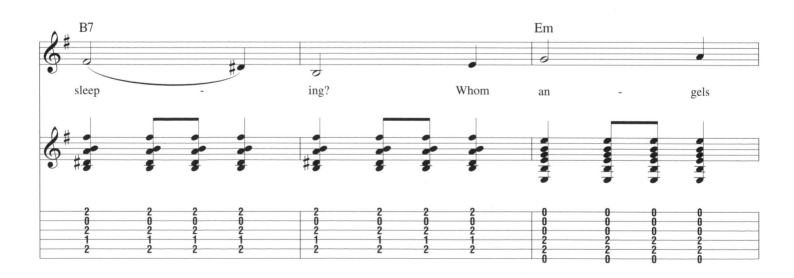

sleep - ing? Whom an - gels

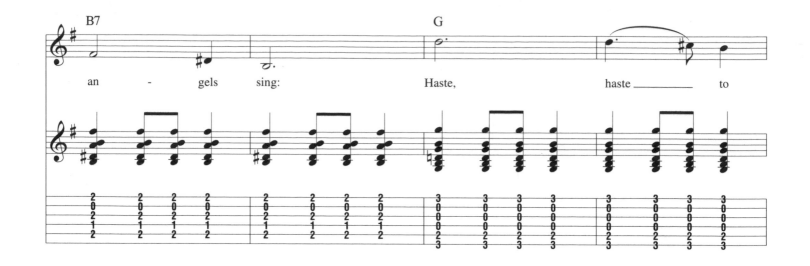

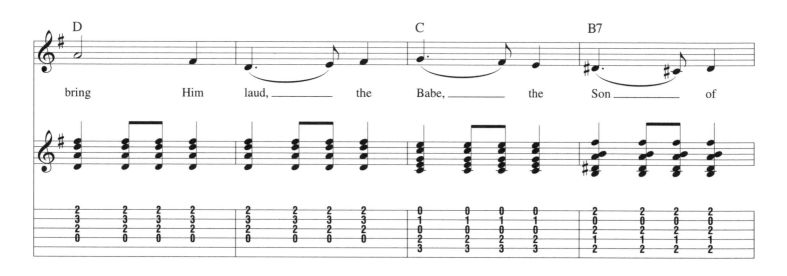

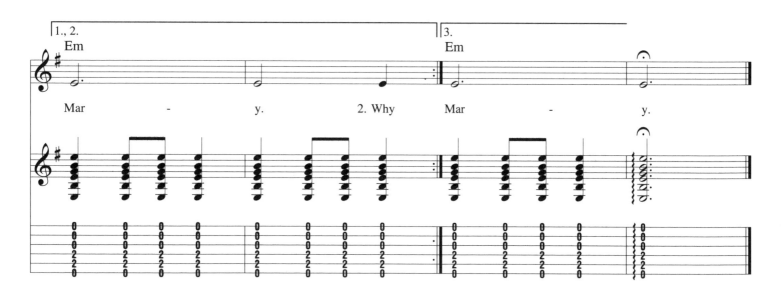

Additional Lyrics

2. Why lies He in such mean estate
   Where ox and ass are feeding?
   Good Christian, fear, for sinners here
   The silent word is pleading.

3. So bring Him incense, gold and myrrh.
   Come, peasant King, to own Him.
   The King of Kings salvation brings,
   Let loving hearts enthrone Him.